AMAZING WINTER OLYMPICS

FREESTYLE SKIING

BY ASHLEY GISH

CREATIVE EDUCATION • CREATIVE PAPERBACKS

Published by Creative Education and Creative Paperbacks
P.O. Box 227, Mankato, Minnesota 56002
Creative Education and Creative Paperbacks are imprints of
The Creative Company
www.thecreativecompany.us

Design by The Design Lab
Production by Rachel Klimpel
Art direction by Rita Marshall
Printed in the United States of America

Photographs by Alamy (dpa picture alliance, PA Images, REUTERS, UPI), AP Images (ASSOCIATED PRESS), Getty Images (Wally McNamee/Corbis Historical), iStockphoto (mbbirdy), Shutterstock (mumbo-jumbo, Iurii Osadchi, Federico Rostagno, TSLPhoto)

Library of Congress Cataloging-in-Publication Data
Names: Gish, Ashley, author.
Title: Freestyle skiing / Ashley Gish.
Series: Amazing Winter Olympics.
Includes bibliographical references and index.
Summary: Celebrate the Winter Games with this high-interest introduction to freestyle skiing, the sport known for its aerial and mogul events. Also included is a biographical story about skier Alexandre Bilodeau.

Identifiers:
ISBN 978-1-64026-495-3 (hardcover)
ISBN 978-1-68277-047-4 (pbk)
ISBN 978-1-64000-625-6 (eBook)
This title has been submitted for CIP processing under LCCN 2021937771.

First Edition HC 9 8 7 6 5 4 3 2 1
First Edition PBK 9 8 7 6 5 4 3 2 1

Table of Contents

Olympic Beginnings 4

Extreme Athletes 7

Freestyle Gear 8

Olympic Events 11

Slopestyle and Big Air 15

Halfpipe and Ski Cross 19

Amazing Freestyle Skiing 20

Competitor Spotlight: Alexandre Bilodeau 22

Read More 24

Websites 24

Index 24

At its first Games, freestyle was a demonstration sport, with winners excluded from the medal count.

A wild new trend began in the 1930s. Skiers soared into the air, doing flips and spins. "Hotdogging," as it was called, caught on quickly. In 1979, the **International Ski Federation** created rules for hotdogging. The sport became known as freestyle. It has been part of the Winter Olympics since 1988.

International Ski Federation Fédération Internationale de Ski (FIS) organizes and sets rules for international winter sports

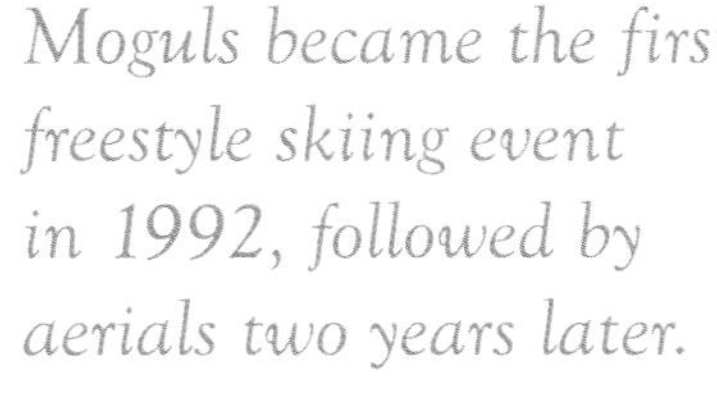

Moguls became the first freestyle skiing event in 1992, followed by aerials two years later.

Freestyle is an extreme sport. It combines speed with style and acrobatics. Freestyle skiers are bold and incredible athletes. In some events, they launch themselves off jumps to fly as high as 50 feet (15.2 m) in the air. Then they spin, flip, and twist before landing gracefully.

acrobatics difficult or dangerous moves

Freestyle skiers wear helmets. Some wear back protection and knee pads. Many use skis that are shorter and lighter than regular ones. Tips on both the front and back help skiers land more daring moves.

The different colors of goggle lenses help skiers see in many weather and lighting conditions.

SUI
AUS
SWEDEN
AUSTRALIA
FRANCE

In ski cross, multiple skiers race together on the same course.

Today, the Winter Games offer six freestyle events. These are **aerials**, moguls, ski slopestyle, big air, ski **halfpipe**, and ski cross. Some skiers compete in more than one event.

aerials acrobatic moves performed in the air by freestyle skiers

halfpipe a track or slope shaped like a pipe cut in half

Aerial skiers zoom off jumps to flip and twist in the air. In moguls, skiers race at top speeds around large snow mounds.

Aerial skiers are judged on their takeoff, form, landing, and the difficulty of their jumps.

PyeongChang 2018
PyeongChang 2018

68

Slopestyle skiers must show both control and skill. They ski through an obstacle course of rails and ramps. The ramps send them into the air, where they do tricks.

Slopestyle skiers focus more on completing the obstacles than on speed.

Big air events call for a bigger ramp. The skier shoots farther into the air for one big jump.

Big air was a new freestyle event added to the Olympics for 2022.

34

ATOMIC
ATOMIC

The halfpipe built for the 2018 Olympics was 64 feet (19.5 m) wide with 22-foot-high (6.7 m) walls.

Halfpipe skiers use the halfpipe's sides to slide into the air. After their tricks, they land and ski up the other side of the pipe to do more! In ski cross, multiple skiers race down a course with jumps and **banks**.

banks piles of packed snow that send skiers into a turn

Highflying freestyle skiers do amazing tricks. Watch this thrilling sport in the next Winter Olympics!

As of 2021, Canada had tallied the most gold medals in freestyle skiing events.

Competitor Spotlight: Alexandre Bilodeau

When Alexandre Bilodeau was young, his family started skiing together. He was not excited at first. But after he watched Jean-Luc Brassard take the gold in 1994, Bilodeau was hooked on freestyle skiing. In 2010, Bilodeau became the first Canadian to win gold in moguls while competing at the Winter Olympics in Vancouver, Canada. He won gold again at the 2014 Olympics.

CANADA
vancouver 2010

Read More

Burns, Kylie. *Alpine and Freestyle Skiing*. New York: Crabtree, 2010.

Carr, Aaron. *Skiing*. New York: Weigl, 2018.

Smith, Elliott. *Freeskiing and Other Extreme Snow Sports*. Mankato, Minn.: Capstone, 2020.

Websites

Bilodeau - Men's Freestyle Skiing - Moguls
https://www.youtube.com/watch?v=4e-TxH7FR4U
Watch Alexandre Bilodeau's gold-medal win at the 2010 Winter Olympics.

Kiddle: Freestyle Skiing Facts for Kids
https://kids.kiddle.co/Freestyle_skiing
Learn about the history and types of freestyle skiing.

Index

Bilodeau, Alexandre 22
events 7, 11
gear 8
halfpipe 11, 19
International Ski Federation 4
jumps 7, 12, 16, 19
medals 22
ramps 15, 16